Green Sea Turtle

by Tom Jackson

Consultants:

John E. McCosker, PhD
Chair of Aquatic Biology, California Academy of Sciences

Maureen Flannery, MS
Ornithology and Mammalogy Collection Manager, California Academy of Sciences

Wallace J. Nichols, PhD
Research Associate, California Academy of Sciences

BEARPORT
PUBLISHING

New York, New York

WOODRIDGE PUBLIC LIBRARY
3 PLAZA DRIVE
WOODRIDGE, IL 60517-5014
(630) 964-7899

D1712141

Credits

Cover, © M. M. Sweet/Getty Images; 3, © iStockphoto/Thinkstock; 4–5, © Chris Newbert/Minden Pictures/FLPA; 6, © Shutterstock; 7, © Norbert Probst/Imagebroker/FLPA; 9, © Michale Sza/NYI/FLPA; 10–11, © Todd Taulman/Shutterstock; 12, © Shutterstock; 13, © iStockphoto/Thinkstock; 14, © Norbert Wu/Minden Pictures/FLPA; 15, © iStockphoto/Thinkstock; 15L, © Tom Middleton/Shutterstock; 15T, © Image Source/Corbis; 15BR, © Mike Parry/Minden Pictures/FLPA; 16, © Mitsuaki Iwago/Minden Pictures/FLPA; 17, © Kevin Schafer/Minden Pictures/FLPA; 18, © Kevin Schafer/Corbis; 19, © M. Harvey/WILDLIFE; 20–21, © Tim Fitzharris/Minden Pictures/FLPA; 22TL, © Shutterstock; 22CL, © iStockphoto/Thinkstock; 22BL, © Kevin Schafer/Corbis; 22TR, © David Everson/Shutterstock; 22CR, © Mitsuaki Iwago/Minden Pictures/FLPA; 22BR, © Juniors Tierbildarchiv/Photoshot; 23TL, © Borisoff/Shutterstock; 23TC, © Rich Carey/Shutterstock; 23TR, © Roger Le Guen/Biosphoto; 23BL, © Blue Orange Studio/Shutterstock; 23BC, © Anna Segeren/Shutterstock; 23BR, © Mikhail Dudarev/Shutterstock.

Publisher: Kenn Goin
Creative Director: Spencer Brinker
Editorial Director: Adam Siegel
Photo Researcher: Brown Bear Books Ltd

Library of Congress Cataloging-in-Publication Data

Jackson, Tom, 1972–
  Green sea turtle / by Tom Jackson.
    p. cm. — (The deep end: animal life underwater)
  Includes bibliographical references and index.
  ISBN-13: 978-1-61772-920-1 (library binding)
  ISBN-10: 1-61772-920-5 (library binding)
  1. Green turtle—Juvenile literature. I. Title.
  QL666.C536J33 2014
  597.92'8—dc23
                    2013011548

For more information, write to Bearport Publishing Company, Inc., 45 West 21st Street, Suite 3B, New York, New York 10010. Printed in the United States of America.

10 9 8 7 6 5 4 3 2 1

Contents

Swimming and Searching

A green sea turtle slowly swims in a **shallow**, warm part of the ocean.

It passes by a **coral reef**.

Then it swims past an area that is covered by soft sand.

As it glides through the water, it looks for sea plants to eat.

What part of a turtle's body helps it stay safe from animals that want to eat it?

Because green sea turtles spend most of their time in shallow water, they are usually found near shore.

green sea turtle

A Strong Shell

A green sea turtle has a shell that covers most of its body.

The shell is very strong.

It's made up of large flat pieces of bone covered by hard skin.

Like a suit of armor, it protects the turtle from animals that try to attack.

hard shell

What parts of a turtle's body help it swim?

A turtle's shell has two parts. The top part is curved, and the bottom part is flat.

curved top

flat bottom

A green sea turtle is built for swimming underwater.

Its four legs are paddle-shaped **flippers**.

To swim, the turtle flaps its long front flippers up and down.

They move like the wings of a bird.

The turtle uses its back flippers for steering.

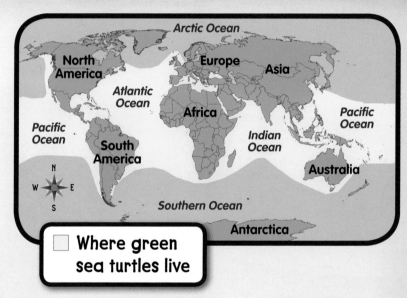

Arctic Ocean

North America

Europe

Asia

Atlantic Ocean

Pacific Ocean

Africa

Indian Ocean

Pacific Ocean

South America

Australia

Southern Ocean

Antarctica

N W E S

☐ Where green sea turtles live

Green sea turtles live and swim in warm ocean waters around the world.

Taking a Breath

A sea turtle spends most of its life in the ocean.

However, it can't breathe underwater.

Instead, it comes to the **surface** to take a deep breath about every five minutes.

A turtle can hold its breath for much longer than that, though.

As it sleeps on the sea floor, it does not breathe for several hours.

sea turtle breathing air

There are about 280 kinds of turtles. Most of them live on land or in freshwater, such as ponds and lakes. However, seven types, including green sea turtles, live in the ocean.

Hungry Sea Turtles

Green sea turtles feed mainly on plants.

They eat sea grasses and seaweeds on the bottom of shallow, sunlit seas.

A turtle does not have teeth to chew food, however.

Instead, it has a sharp beak.

The beak works like a scissors to slice off mouthfuls of food.

beak

How do you think people who fish with nets could be dangerous to turtles?

A sea turtle's beak is made from the same material as a person's hair and fingernails.

beak

sea grass

A Turtle's Enemies

A sea turtle has few enemies in the ocean.

Only crocodiles, killer whales, and some kinds of sharks are strong enough to crack its shell.

Sea turtles face a bigger danger from people, however.

Every year, many turtles are accidentally trapped in fishing nets.

Some people also hunt and eat sea turtles.

sea turtle caught in a fishing net

Today, green sea turtles are in danger of dying out. Scientists think there are fewer than 200,000 of them in the world.

Green Sea Turtle Enemies

killer whale

shark

crocodile

15

Laying Eggs

Male sea turtles rarely leave the ocean.

Females leave the water for only one reason—to lay eggs.

Every two or three years, a female pulls herself onto a sandy beach at night.

Using her back flippers, she digs a hole in the sand and lays up to 150 eggs.

Then she buries the eggs to keep them safe and returns to the water.

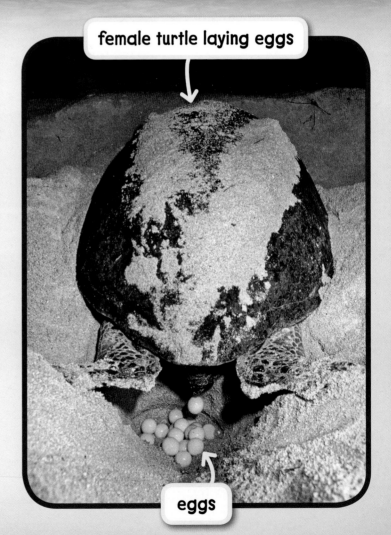

female turtle laying eggs

eggs

Sea turtles lay their eggs on land because the babies inside the eggs would drown if they **hatched** underwater.

female turtle burying eggs

How do you think baby sea turtles get back to the ocean?

Racing to the Water

After about 60 days, baby turtles hatch from their eggs.

They dig themselves out of their sandy nest.

Then, at night, they move as fast as they can over the sand and into the sea.

This trip is very dangerous for the **hatchlings**.

Many of them never reach the water because seabirds and crabs grab and eat them.

turtle hatching

baby turtles racing to the sea

Turtle hatchlings are tiny—only about four inches (10 cm) long.

A Lifetime at Sea

Unlike adult green sea turtles, young turtles live far out at sea.

They catch and eat jellyfish, shrimps, worms, and other sea creatures.

As they grow bigger, however, they move to shallow, sunlit places.

There, they spend the rest of their lives—swimming slowly as they search for food.

A green sea turtle can grow to be three or four feet (1 or 1.2 m) long and weigh around 400 pounds (181 kg). It can live for up to 80 years in the wild.

Science Lab

Be a Sea Turtle Scientist

Imagine you are a scientist who studies green sea turtles.

Look at these pictures and see if you can figure out what the turtles are doing.

Then use the pictures to tell your friends and family what you learned about green sea turtles.

(The answers are on page 24.)

Science Words

coral reef (KOR-uhl REEF) a group of structures formed from the skeletons of sea animals called coral polyps

flippers (FLIP-urz) front and back limbs on a sea turtle's body that help it move and steer

hatched (HACHT) when an animal comes out of an egg

hatchlings (HACH-lings) baby animals, such as turtles, that have just come out of their eggs

shallow (SHAL-oh) not very deep

surface (SUR-fiss) the top layer of something, such as an ocean or river

Index

Read More

Marsh, Laura. *Sea Turtles (National Geographic Readers).* Washington, D.C.: National Geographic (2011).

Rhodes, Mary Jo, and David Hall. *Sea Turtles (Undersea Encounters).* New York: Scholastic (2005).

Weber, Valerie. *Sea Turtles (Animals That Live in the Ocean).* Pleasantville, NY: Weekly Reader (2009).

Learn More Online

To learn more about green sea turtles, visit **www.bearportpublishing.com/TheDeepEnd**

Answers for Page 22

1. Swimming in the sea; 2. Digging a nest in the sand or burying eggs;
3. Eating sea grass; 4. Laying eggs; 5. Hatching from an egg; 6. Racing to the ocean

About the Author

Tom Jackson learned about animals in college and has worked in zoos, African safari parks, and rain forests. He now writes books about natural history and science in his attic in England.